A Fold in the Map

ISOBEL DIXON was born in Umtata and grew up in the Karoo region of South Africa. Her debut collection *Weather Eye* (Carapace, 2001) won the Sanlam and the Olive Schreiner Prizes. Her work has appeared in two pamphlets, *Unfold* (2002) and *Ask For It By Name* (2007), produced by a group of London-based poets. She has also been published in the *New Writing* anthologies, *The Paris Review*, *The Guardian*, and *London Magazine*, among others, and been translated into Dutch and Turkish. She lives in Cambridge.

Also by Isobel Dixon

Weather Eye (2001)

A Fold in the Map

Isobel Dixon

For Cathy,

from another daughter,
with warmest wishes
& in memory of another
fine father, Wulf.

Isobel

28.6.12

SALT

CAMBRIDGE

PUBLISHED BY SALT PUBLISHING
14a High Street, Fulbourn, Cambridge CB21 5DH United Kingdom

First published 2007
Reprinted 2008

Printed and bound in Great Britain by Biddles Ltd, King's Lynn, Norfolk

Typeset in Swift 9.5 / 13

ISBN 978 1 84471 396 7 hardback

Salt Publishing Ltd gratefully acknowledges
the financial assistance of Arts Council England

1 3 5 7 9 8 6 4 2

For my mother
&
in memory of my mother,
who loved a good map.

And with love and thanks
to Jan
who brought my passport
when it mattered most.

Contents

Acknowledgements

Some of the poems in this collection have appeared in the following publications: *A Literary Guide to the Eastern Cape*, *Ask for It by Name*, *Automatic Lighthouse: Tall Lighthouse Poetry Review*, *Avocado*, *Birds in Words: A Twitcher's Guide to South African Poetry*, *Carapace*, *CIE Poetry Anthology*, *City in Words: An Anthology of Cape Town Poems*, *Die Hören*, *Imagination in a Troubled Space: A South African Poetry Reader*, *In the Criminal's Cabinet*, *Journal of Post-Colonial Writing*, *LitNet*, *London Magazine*, *New Coin*, *New Contrast*, *New Writing 10*, *New Writing 11*, *nthposition*, *Oxfam 'Poems for a Better Future'*, *Poetry 2000*, *somewhere*, *Scrutiny2*, *Unfold*, *Voices From All Over*, *Wasafiri*, *Weather Eye*, *The Wolf*.

My thanks are due to the editors of these journals and anthologies, and to the English Academy of Southern Africa and the sponsors and judges of the Sanlam Prize and the Olive Schreiner Prize. There are several poets whose friendship and poetic instincts have helped to make the publication of two joint pamphlets, *Unfold* and *Ask For It By Name*, such a great pleasure—warm thanks to Helen Clare, Olivia Cole, Andrew Dilger, Luke Heeley, Liane Strauss, Roisin Tierney, and especially to Simon Barraclough. I am also grateful to Clive James for including my work on the guest poets' pages of his website, to Ilyas Tunc for translating some of these poems into Turkish, and to Jan Morris for the inspiration for the title.

The quote from *The Emigrants* by W.G. Sebald, published by Harvill Press, is reprinted by permission of The Random House Group Ltd.

Plenty

Plenty

When I was young and there were five of us,
all running riot to my mother's quiet despair,
our old enamel tub, age-stained and pocked
upon its griffin claws, was never full.

Such plenty was too dear in our expanse of drought
where dams leaked dry and windmills stalled.
Like Mommy's smile. Her lips stretched back
and anchored down, in anger at some fault—

of mine, I thought—not knowing then
it was a clasp to keep us all from chaos.
She saw it always, snapping locks and straps,
the spilling: sums and worries, shopping lists

for aspirin, porridge, petrol, bread.
Even the toilet paper counted,
and each month was weeks too long.
Her mouth a lid clamped hard on this.

We thought her mean. Skipped chores,
swiped biscuits—best of all
when she was out of earshot
stole another precious inch

up to our chests, such lovely sin,
lolling luxuriant in secret warmth
disgorged from fat brass taps,
our old compliant co-conspirators.

Now bubbles lap my chin. I am a sybarite.
The shower's a hot cascade
and water's plentiful, to excess, almost, here.
I leave the heating on.

And miss my scattered sisters,
all those bathroom squabbles and, at last,
my mother's smile, loosed from the bonds
of lean, dry times and our long childhood.

Weather Eye

In summer when the Christmas beetles
filled each day with thin brass shrilling,
heat would wake you, lapping at the sheet,
and drive you up and out into the glare
to find the mulberry's deep shade
or watch ants marching underneath the guava tree.

And in the house Mommy would start
the daily ritual, whipping curtains closed,
then shutters latched against the sun
and when you crept in, thirsty, from the garden,
the house would be a cool, dark cave,

an enclave barricaded against light
and carpeted with shadow, still
except the kitchen where the door was open
to nasturtiums flaming at the steps
while on the stove the pressure cooker chugged
in tandem with the steamy day.

And in the evenings when the sun had settled
and crickets started silvering the night,
just home from school, smelling of chalk and sweat,
Daddy would do his part of it, the checking,
on the front verandah, of the scientific facts.

Then if the temperature had dropped enough
the stays were loosened and the house undressed
for night. Even the front door wide now
for the slightest breeze, a welcoming
of all the season's scents, the jasmine,
someone else's supper, and a neighbour's voice—

out walking labradors, the only time of day
for it, this time of year. How well the world
was ordered then. These chill machines
don't do it half as true, the loving regulation
of the burning days. Somehow my judgment isn't quite
as sure when faced with weather-signs. Let me come home
to where you watch the skies and keep things right.

For Ann and Harwood

Crossing

Old men with beards remind me of my father:
surplice white, a beard of blessing,
Father Christmas face.

I just can't help but smile at them,
old rabbi daddies, walking in the street.

My dad will tip his hat at everyone
he meets—old-fashioned courtesy—
now leaning slightly on his stick.

Does he greet dark-haired daughters too,
with just a touch of extra love?

Come to this city then and see me weave
among the crowds that beat
these concrete pavements every day.

(You'll never have the time to greet them all,
these urgent hurriers.)

But tap-tap slowly to the kerb, hold up your staff
against the iron roar, and when the wood leaps
in your hand, strike at the tar.

There'll be a stillness as the faultline fissures
deeper than the Underground.

The engines stop, the hush reminding us
of history and grace.
The clear 'good morning' from your smiling face
settling among us like a dove.

Christmas Beetles

Outside, the afternoon is ringing,
ringing, massed cicadas singing out
their silly news. The hot
brown garden's loud
with all their gossipmongering.

The insect grapevine—
shrill bush telephone—
incessant beetle headlines
shrieked into the heat.

Like our old radiogram,
its fizzing, whistling, wheezing,
as we ease the big ribbed knob
and line the red bar up,
with news from Moscow, Greece,
Lourenço Marques.

These noisy chaps are closer,
sounding off from somewhere near.
The jacaranda, or the orange trees,
we can't be sure.
They are everywhere,
and nowhere, sly cicadas,
no-one can decipher them.

Or was it just the sound
of sticky tarmac, shimmering?
Who knows? Perhaps the noonday shouting
never was that clamorous.
Our tricky memory contrives
and always turns the volume up

and in the end I guess
that they were merely stuck
at fundamentals, needle jumping
at the prod of sex, or simply whooping
—*summer! summer! summer!*—
every minute of their short, hot, beetle lives.

Amanzi

Outside the panes of jewelled glass
the rain pours down. How strange
to think my childhood years were marked
by prayers for rain. Here there's no need.
So very little need at all, it seems.
No question of it, all the grass is greener
here. The lawns of Cambridge, emerald,
manicured, this town's inhabitants secure
in cosy, educated affluence and peace.

Days later, home, I see new boxy houses
and a sign: *Joe Slovo Township*. And a shop,
the *Bright Life Store*, with its own homemade
logo praising *Coke*. In Table Mountain's
richer shade, the phrasing *Armed Response*
is echoed, wall to whitewashed wall.
Down at the lights, I stop at red and shake my head
at all the kids who weave between the cars,
come tapping on the glass. But one
holds out his windmill made from wire and tin,
its spinning blades reminding me of long hot roads,
and dusty plains. Of being young and prayers for rain.
It costs ten rand, a pound. I wind the window down.

A View of Empire from a Train

Who positioned these perfect black-and-white cows
in the landscape (the gently rolling fields
of English Christmas present calendars)?
Like the Timpo Toys we carefully arranged
on a green felt spread far lusher
than the veld we ever had,
some smoothed-out foil or broken mirror
for that glassy pond.

Back then, from small beginnings—
shipwreck, orphanhood—
we'd build a homestead, sprawling ranch,
a village, then a dynasty
as the milking girl with the boots and bucket
married (of course, how else?)
the suave black-stetsonned cowboy man,
and they, and all the wild and farmyard animals, bred.

Things multiply. The story ran for weeks.
But we'd get bored with such abundance,
our mother raging about all the mess,
and so we'd plan a *devastating* end to all of it:
rid of the burden of creation, all those lives.
At last, the pure relief of *Finis*:
    volcano, fire or flood.
The promise, later in the holiday
we might just start again, Year Zero.

The Skinning

I watched my older cousin skin a mole:
it seemed a fearsome thing to do, but I was eager
to be big and full of knowledge, so I stayed there,
brave girl, hunkered down, my flowered skirt
rucked up between my summer knees.
The shed's stone step—his rough autopsy table—
pressed the morning's gathered heat into my soles,
the same heat rising through the opened body
of the mole. I frowned against the boomerang
of sun, flung, swerving, off the blade at me,
and in the quiet of the early afternoon—the grown-ups
at their ritual naps—the whispering, *skrrt-skrrt*,
skin peeling back as if from velvet fruit, rasped
louder than the new, enormous thudding of my heart.

No bigger than a mango really, it had fitted in his palm
after the shot, a trophy for his patience, waiting, poised,
brave backyard hunter, ready finger on the trigger lip.
Unsuspecting, it had snuffled to the ceiling of the lawn,
a creature from a picture book, old Mouldiwarp: soft snout,
a pair of small, intrepid claws, a grubby engineer
whose only fault was choosing my aunt's emerald pride
and joy as his back door. But now it lay as dumb
as fruit, and leaking juice, a thick and sweethot scent
I had to suck my teeth against—but no, I wouldn't
look away, or pinch my nose, as his brown fingers,
almost priestly, probed the tight-packed inner things.
I watched, and didn't flinch: his certainty and skill—
and then his sudden, flashing grin, conspiratorial,
as though I wasn't just a scaredy-cat who couldn't catch
a ball or swim: I'd crouched to skin a mole with him,
and so I too, accomplice now, was in on his small kill.

Shaken from Her Sleep

A girl wakes in the night. The room
is trembling and at first she thinks
it's just her anxiousness, a dream,
the heat — her boyfriend's t-shirt clinging
damply to her skin. He's gone,
left on the train, just yesterday,
called up for Basics. (Now, in camp,
he's polishing his boots and trying
not to cry.) The cloth still smells of him.

She goes out on the balcony
to breathe, to stop the midnight quake,
but finds it waiting for her
in the humid dark. A coming
storm, steel banks of clouds advancing,
thundering? But no, the drought's
not broken yet. The streets are dry
and she can see Orion's Belt,
the jewelled sword poised in the sky

above the town, the plain. Can he see
it too, where he is — hair shorn, close
to his skull, that handsome head,
caressed and loved, laid in her lap?
Leaning on the rail, she gulps
in air, to drown the ache, and feels
the metal shiver in her grip.
Through the trees, down at the crossing,
she now spies the cause: a convoy,

giant tortoises, lumbering, down
the main street, to the church.
Will the spire shake too as they pass,
head for the town hall and the park
where the angel stands, raising
her sword above the lost sons' names?
Soft summer nights, he'd steal the roses
planted in their memory, for her,
without a thought. But now the world

is real, though she can't make sense
of those distant wars and this night's
visitation, how they fit, or not.
In these small hours they loom immense,
slow, clumsy creatures hiding keen,
ferocious cleverness. But in
the sunshine of Commando Day
they'll seem much tamer, as the children
clamber over the displays and fathers

marvel at design, 'in spite
of sanctions', talk of threat calmed
by this show of powerful
defence. But now she lies down, hopes
her heart's mad drum will let her sleep
again. Disturbed, she's not sure what
she fears the most: what's outside
all she knows; or that their love,
her silence, and this little, peaceful
town, are neat, efficient levers
in some terrible machine.

Foreshadow

I set myself this task:
walk home from school on shadows—
not something to be lightly
undertaken, noon in the Karoo,
sun blazing high and vertical,
and shadows scarce.

It cost long, slow diversions
down the tree-lined streets, huge leaps
to where the dappled stipplings
of the leaves proved only just enough
and one brief foray into someone's
garden and the fretted path

cast by a lucky willow tree.
At last, red-faced and sticky,
squeezed into the margin—
thin black line thrown to the pavement
by a gutterpipe—I wrestled
with my laces, stripped off

dust-embroidered socks and stepped
down to the furrow's cool
and fluid seam. My suitcase,
burdensome with schoolbooks, hoisted
to my head: a Congo porter,
knee-deep, stoic, wading home.

No hero's welcome though:
my footprints barely drying
on the flagstones, our verandah,
and the silence of the house
already ominous. My sisters
long returned, lunch eaten,

dishes washed. How could I know
she would be phoning, frantic—
my mother, always unconcerned,
sending me out on testing errands,
making me grow up brave. How to explain
this silly shadow-play?

As if I had a choice—
did she think I went on it,
that thirsty journey, just to vex her,
that I wanted to come home to scolding,
hot and dusty, hours late?
Didn't she understand

that once you've set out on your odyssey
you're bound to it, to rules you cannot break?

For Gus

Certus Incertus

Noon classroom heat, the rhyme a perfect whole
shaped in her head, the air
as heavy as a drape about her

as she stands, the clever one,
her hands pressed hot against her skirt.
Then dumb-show swallowing

and mime. The rapid fire of cocked-up consonants.
The stretching out of time—
A sentence come unstrung. And no escape.

God wove humility into my tongue,
stitched knots into its root:
words made my stumbling blocks

and snares. Both gift and downfall,
so a syllable could catch me unawares
despite the careful path

I'd laid about the difficult.
Alone, a poem was paradise.
Aloud, an ambuscade.

And still my name is treacherous:
the first an easy swim,
a sibilance, soft labial,

and then warm lateral rest.
A stubborn plosive bars the last,
refusing. The mouth's tough muscle trapped,

a clumsy toad that's scarred and furrowed
as if mapped with all its failed assaults,
the long embarrassments

as listeners' lips chew silently,
rehearsing what they think I mean.
Pace! I've better words inside than these —

gladly abandon sound bytes
and embrace the peace of foolscap,
the pleasure of a faintly humming screen.

Gemini

Below my heart hang two pale women,
ghostly, gelid, sea-horse girls.
Without my telling you would never
see them, tiny tapioca clumps suspended
in the silt between my bones.

So nearly motionless, they are both breathing,
dreaming their amoebic dreams,
and I swear when I wake before dawn, try
vainly to return to mine, I hear them, faintly,
murmuring. But my ribs make a shallow hull

and one of them must go. Duck, bail out,
flushed into the sewage and the wider sea.
I can't endure them both, adrift
among my vital parts, sizing each other up
with tadpole eyes. I must decide

and feed the lucky one. Let the other shrink,
dissolve back to this body's salty soup.
Look closely at them: soulmates, secret
sharers, not-quite-siamese. Who stays,
who goes, which one of them is history?

She kicks up an almighty storm, makes
waves, enormous, tidal; while her sister's
calm, pacific, dull. Our oil-on-troubled-water-
pourer, keeper of the peace. You choose —
mark one who should be squeezed out

of this narrow vessel; voided, spilled,
to lighten, buoy me, make some space.
Plain sailing then, I'll forge ahead, forget
her spectral presence, and a lifetime's
sly, subversive whispering. Learn

single-mindedness at last. But when it's well
and truly done, how will I know? Will I feel
relief, release, how the balance shifts
and settles; then walk straight, unpuzzled,
sure—or limp and stumble, still
obscurely troubled, phantom-limbed?

Positano

The villa's whitewash clotted
scarlet with geraniums,
the bougainvillea's purple
bruise smeared inbetween—
I sit here, mottled,
in the shadow of the vine.
The sea is welded
to the sky, a beaten
shield, enamelled, glittering
and everything is molten,
rich, beneath this sun,
such grandiose munificence,
the alchemy transforming
even me—slowly, in thrall,
from milk to gold. After
a day among the ruins
of Pompeii, dust still clings,
a pale reminder, to my shoes,
but now I watch the yachts
below and ring the ice against
the bottom of my glass,
an answer to the winking sea,
the tinkling of the masts.
Remember Ripley, wish
I didn't wish for all of this
and more. This lustrous,
postcard life. Hear
how my darkened hallway's
silence shudders at the falling
to the mat, implacable,
of crisp, clear-windowed
envelopes, that smother
my bright rectangle,
its foreign stamp,
the lines I sent back

to my dull domestic self:
Wish you were dead,
and I was always whole
and golden, always here.

(I Want) Something to Show for It

I'm not the kind who treasures
love notes in the sand, laid bare
for the lobstered swimsuit mob

to stare at, for the tide to lick
away. I want a token,
solid, in my hand. Something

with staying power, not easily lost
or broken. Do you understand?
You murmur, puzzled by my greed,

"What is *it* that you want a thing
to show for, anyway?" You may
well ask. It's just a zero,

universal emptiness. It
brings forth nothing except need,
and the truth is, souvenirs

won't do the trick: no poseur
snaps, no neat, insipid
diaries, no sickly rock,

unusual pebbles, musty shells. I want
the shining cliffs, the posh hotel,
the whole shebang. The waiters

running across emerald lawns,
their heavy silver platters
raised in skilful hands. I want

the tacky postcard carousels,
the smugly clinking tills, the dumpy
women sweating at their counters

every summer, summer-long,
as well. I want their oily husbands
grinning now from ear to ear—

I am the sea come to swallow the pier.

The Root of It

Morning glories' extraordinary purple's
only for the vine.
Once plucked the trumpets shrivel up
like spent balloons,
the morning after everything.

And pebbles, lifted from the river, dry
and lose their lustre,
weigh our pockets down. Sour-smelling
sea-shells, pillaged
from the beach, once pearled with light.

Though I believe what's lost in the translation
keeps on whispering
to us in dreams. The tongue's root holds.
But how to find
a waking voice, and honest lungs

that I can trust to speak of my own place,
and how to trace
that most elusive source: the ocean,
riverbed or stem?
How not to be a specimen,

impaled, damaged, adrift. The journey's cost,
the richness gained
at what expense. The rift between the past
and this. How speech
evades us, how our longing hearts dry up.

Kudu Watch

Signs bloom mysterious,
loom sudden, briefly luminous,
moonflowers edged in red.

Our lights create the road,
its unremitting dashes are
a pale Morse code, monotonous,

as I count the kilometres
mesmerised. Keep watch,
still far to go. We are taking it slow

tonight, this lonely stretch
notorious for lulling
the unwary to unbroken rest.

Here in the passenger seat
I feel the night's weight,
the need to press back sleep,

for both our sakes and for those
who wait for us. My mother
baking, changing sheets, preparing,

wearing herself out with tense
expectancy. Through my own
long-journey weariness

I try to reckon all the years
I've known this road, the stories
of its spectral hitchhiker—

how I felt for her, bleak shade
endlessly thumbing useless rides,
always en route. And now

with this tar, and all of Africa
between my homes and sisters
I am back on midnight guard:

eyes peeled for chalky markings
on a granite pelt, the phosphor flare
of light reflected on a startled eye,

a stirring on the verge, a muscled
gathering: strange that a gently
grazing herbivore can, leaping, be

death's angel here. I feel the world
relies on my night vigilance,
ever-alert. Who could see

that my vision of anxiety
is not the buck clearing the fence,
but the devastating consequence

of a smaller body crashing
through the screen's transparency,
how worlds collide:

Woman Shatters Windscreen,
Exploding From Inside.

Strike Softly Away from the Body

Is it the kleptomaniac fire-starter in me,
or my mother's thrift
that makes me reach for them so greedily:
free flipped books of flattened organ pipes,
the neatly sliding drawers of flares?

Knowing my whim, you come to the pub
with your snaffled gift:
Wild-Life series 2: sub-Dürer-print rhinoceros.
A beast to add to the array I feed the stove,
the braai, my scattered candles with.

This is the light my mother claims to hate—
the gloom of poverty
not soft romance. Here, my domain
after the flickering day, the pixelled screen,
the speeding fluorescent carriage of the train.

Shaking them up, my cheap maracas,
irresistible,
I am duly warned: DANGER! FIRE KILLS
CHILDREN (and not grown-ups?), with a moon-
faced stickman, gaping, asymmetrically aflame,

to make quite sure the point is driven home;
recalling terrible
tales of girls in rayon nightdresses, the hearth-
fire horrors summoned up to caution us.
And how, despite all this, as backyard Musketeers

or Indians (I can't remember which) we set
the wendy-house on fire:
really just a sideways heirloom shipping crate,
tar-paper lined. All the aunts and uncles
carrying buckets from the tap, as the flames lapped

at the dried fans of our garden's palm.
But I still desire,
after all these warning signs, the sulphur scratch,
the bright corona lighting tip to wick—
even the burned-down splinter's finger scorch.

And I'm left wondering at this advice,
and what inspired it:
Do Not Place Spent Matches in Box. Safety?
Order? Pure aesthetics? Who can tell.
I blow one out, and disobey; fizz another
bright-lit match-girl vision up, stow
its charred torch with the pristine ranks as well.

Back in the Benighted Kingdom

I'm sorry to see
my mosquito bumps fade:
the love bites of a continent,
marks of its hot embrace.

If anything is dark,
it's this damp island
with its sluggish days,
its quieter, subtler ways
of drawing blood.

She Comes Swimming

She comes swimming to you, following
da Gama's wake. The twisting Nile
won't take her halfway far enough.

No, don't imagine sirens—mermaid
beauty is too delicate and quick.
Nor does she have that radiance,

Botticelli's Venus glow. No golden
goddess, she's a southern
selkie-sister, dusky otter-girl

who breasts the cold Benguela, rides
the rough Atlantic swell, its chilly
tides, for leagues and leagues.

Her pelt is salty, soaked. Worn out,
she floats, a dark Ophelia, thinking
what it feels like just to sink

caressed by seaweed, nibbled by
a school of jewel-plated fish.
But with her chin tipped skyward

she can't miss the Southern Cross
which now looks newly down on her,
a buttress for the roof of her familiar

hemisphere. She's nearly there.
With wrinkled fingertips, she strokes
her rosary of ivory, bone and horn

and some black seed or stone
she can't recall the name of,
only knows its rubbed-down feel.

And then she thanks her stars,
the ones she's always known,
and flips herself, to find her rhythm

and her course again. On, southwards,
yes, much further south than this.
This time she'll pay attention

to the names—not just the English,
Portuguese and Dutch, the splicings
and accretions of the years. She'll search

for first names in that Urworld, find
her heart-land's mother tongue.
Perhaps there's no such language,

only touch—but that's at least a dialect
still spoken there. She knows when she
arrives she'll have to learn again,

so much forgotten, lost. And when
they put her to the test she fears
she'll be found wanting, out of step.

But now what she must do is swim,
stay focused on each stroke,
until she feels the landshelf

far beneath her rise, a gentle slope
up to the rock, the Cape,
the Fairest Cape. Her Mother City

and its mountain, waiting, wrapped
in veils of cloud and smoke.
Then she must concentrate, dodge

nets and wrack, a plastic bag afloat—
a flaccid, shrunk albino ray—
until she's close enough to touch

down on the seabed, stumble
to the beach—the glistening sand
as great a treasure as her Milky Way—

fall on her knees and plant a kiss
and her old string of beads,
her own explorer's cross

into the cruel, fruitful earth at last.
She's at your feet. Her heart
is beating fast. Her limbs are weak.

Make her look up. Tell her she's home.
Don't send her on her way again.

The Growing Gift

You've no idea, those proteas
you gave me—somehow scavenged bunch—
how those huge soft-furred goblet flowers,
are travelling with me, still.

There was a time I wouldn't have thanked you
for such stubborn heads: hard-hearted,
stiffly-ranged, supremely practical,
the nationalists' tough bloom—

I hated them, so vulgarly
indigenous. Now, roses, snowdrops,
hollyhocks, yes, these were flowers
one could call beautiful,

would plant and nurture, even twist
into your hair. These are too huge
and dense for that. What use are they—
unscented, heavy, blunt?

You filled my arms with them, that night,
the upstairs restaurant. You made
the waitress light a fire against
the Cape's mild winter,

warm and beautiful enough for me,
the wrong end of my holiday
back home. But I was glad of it,
light leaping to our table,

how the fire kept answering your gift,
its milder glow—still flames propped
in a silver bucket—as we laughed,
speaking in Afrikaans

and English, hardly thinking which
was which. Past midnight, then,
my B & B's prim basin swelled,
a southern coronation,

an astonishment. In daylight
I leaned over them, using—your word—
aandagtigheid, attentiveness;
slowly absorbing

all that I had missed, their delicate
geometries. The untranslated
captures it: at once both felted,
soft, yet also guttural:

the palate tongued, first slowly, then
a final snap, and in-between
a purring, gently, in the throat.
The woody stems, those rose-

tipped assegais, the pale cream
inner cone, with fronds as tender
as lambs' eyelashes. I stood there,
on the chilly, gleaming

tiles, stroking the hearts of flowers.
I couldn't bring them back with me;
even such silent aliens
are dangerous. I chose

to split them—single sticks holding
their own exploding heads—left them
with loved ones, who, familiar,
might also feel contempt.

But I'm a convert now. Treasure
my photograph, a clumsy shot
that lops me at the knees, but shows
what matters: mammoth blooms

cupped in my arms. The elbow crooked,
as when I'm pictured cradling
my godchild niece; the weight about
the same. So are we anchored,

always, even from afar. So,
in the night, scented with roses here,
I feel the tug—those ancient stems,
breathing a fragrant sap,
come reaching down my spine.

For Marlene

Meet My Father

Meet My Father

Meet my father, who refuses food —
pecks at it like a bird or not at all —
the beard disguising his thin cheeks.
This, for a man whose appetite was legend,
hoovering up the scraps his daughters couldn't eat.

The dustbin man, we joked.
And here he is, trailing his fork
through food we've laboured to make soft,
delicious, sweet. Too salty, or too tough,
it tastes of nothing, makes him choke,
he keeps insisting, stubbornly.
In truth, the logic's clear. His very life
is bitter and the spice it lacks is hope.
He wants to stop. Why do we keep on
spooning dust and ashes down his throat?

Father

Crossing the threshold of a foreign church,
I step right into you, cheek pressed
against your cassock's folds.
It is the scent, the hush, the candled gloom,
that shrinks me, little girl again,
head bent for blessing, harboured
by the cupola of your large hand.

Just let the children come.
But it was easy then and now I'm old enough
to understand, to taste the sweet, dark cup,
the dry moon melting on my tongue.
We're both too old for childish comfortings,
the certainties of laps and rhymes,
your teaching me, knelt at my bedside,
how to pray. And I, who have much more
to pray for, seem to know much less.
Want intercession, shelter,
if not innocence, then ignorance at least.

Wilful, not quite prodigal, but far away,
I want to be the daughter at the feast
and you, best father,
be the ever-joyful host—never Elijah,
with his ready, empty chair, the absent guest.

Long Distance

Someone's pretending to be Daddy,
speaking with a muffled voice,
low, thick with pain.
It's that old trick, the handkerchief
pressed to the lips. A poor disguise.

Who let this fool impostor take the line?
Put Daddy on the phone again,
so he can chatter on
about some Roman road or ruin,
some funny thing he's read.

Say something now. This intercontinental call
is precious, seconds count.
I gabble words into the time lag,
hear the echo bounce, all nuance lost.
I close my eyes and hope this static silence
simply means the wires are crossed.

Tear

The phone is a cruel mouthpiece,
pain's propaganda tool. A megaphone
for our confusion, for the rest
only delivering half.

My cheerful voice reverberates
until he thinks I've gone, the battery's dead,
and cuts the call. After the click
I let my choked throat spill,
go whimpering around the house,
folding up clothes.

The tickling on the inside of my thigh
becomes a wash of blood.
I stare with dumb eyes at the towel's stain—
it's not my time, my bleeding's past.
I must have wept my insides raw:
stigmata for my father
and his panel-beaten heart.

In the Wind

Walking back, I can't contain myself.
I think too much of Daddy
and must stuff my scarf, a fist of silk,
into my mouth to stop a wail.
It's choked into a whimper,
a spate of fierce, small breaths
as others pass me, going home.
I drop my head. My hair is mercifully
blown across my face and I keep
concentrating madly on the cracks
until I reach the open space:
Midsummer Common in its bitter wind.
My body takes the thrust and slice—
I'm almost glad of its assault
against the skin, the way it strips
the salty dampness from my cheeks
and in a fit of swift bravado
rushes in to tug and lift
the crumpled scarf, whipping it up
above my head, a purpled flame,
battering wildly against the icy dark.
I think of maybe letting go,
not trying to loop the knot again—
watching my colours flying up and out,
unevenly, over the river, into this night.

Listening to the Birds

I can't remember who it was who told me
that to hear the hadedah was sure good luck
but I was wanting to believe it
when I heard the call—lone, double-arced—
within an hour of my own flight's
arrival in the heat.

And then again, down at the coast
another ibis, solemn harbinger:
picking its way, long-billed and serious,
through the uncut grass
below my aunt's wire scrawl of washing line—
my mother's bras flap-flapping there
despondently with hers.
This time the silence gave me hope.

I saw him twice. He seemed lugubrious,
but wise, and once above the hospital
I heard his cousins calling too—
half mocking laugh, half longing cry.
Fierce in belief, these signs weighed more
than any doctor's carefully measured calm.

Now, staring at my plastic cup
of canteen tea grown cold
and filmed with pale grey skin,
I'm trying not to think of those two crows:
huge wings like paper scorched,
black gloss, jerk-stepping their stiff path
across the empty parking lot,
and coughing up dark words.

My Father's Pain

A bright red jacket
stitched with fiery seams,
too small, too tight
and squeezing him,
pressing the breath
out of his wheezing lungs.

To see an old man suffering
is much to bear.
I'm young and strong:
give me that dreadful suit to wear.

Lamb

We left him sleeping peaceful in the night
but they have tied him down, bony wrists
wrapped in a sheepskin cuff, lashed tightly to the rail.

He was fierce after we left, they say:
shouting, tearing at the drip. Hard to believe it
of this gentle man, but this morning,

unbound for the time we're there, he cavils,
clawing at the needle in his arm, moaning
and stubborn, baring his teeth at us

when we refuse. I stroke his fettered hand,
his paper forehead, murmur comfort,
courage, anything. He shakes me off, tossing

his head, red-eyed, an angry ram. Ha!
I must remember who I am: his child,
just a child, why do I question him?

So I hold my tongue, but stay. Lift up the cup,
with its candy-striped concertina straw,
to his splintered lip and he, in resignation, sucks.

Yes, we make a meagre congregation, father,
disobedient. The flesh, indeed, is weak.
Still, remembered echoes of his sermons come:

a promised child, the tangled ram, the sheep-clothed son;
last-minute rescues, legacies, and lies.
The promised and the chosen, certain hopes.

How, from these stories, are we to be wise?
His word was clear and sure before, but now
his raging, rambling, shakes this listener's heart.

And yet, to be here, of some small use,
is a kind of peace. Three spoons of food,
oil for his hands, his feet. Then at last,
at last, returning to gentleness, he sleeps.

Struggle

The matron's jaw is clenched,
her mouth sealed tight. Reluctantly,
she tears a narrow smile from it.
A line slit with a paperknife.

We're locked in battle.
This is her proud vessel,
she's the captain of this ship
and now my father's under her command.
We're nothing to her
but a band of stowaways,
ornery women, rocking the boat.
I half expect she'll send us packing,
off to scrub the deck,
these endless, polished passageways.
But no, I'm staying by his side, on watch.

He lies between us, sleeping,
covered by a sheet.
Across this ravaged territory
I meet her prim, efficient gaze.
I note a flicker—yes, she knows
there's more of us—my sisters,
bold as pirates, tireless, brave.
At last, I see the titan give.

Stay, then, she says.

Singsong

Sleepless, I have gone a little mad,
following my father's footsteps.
Words ricochet. I fill my mind
with drivel, count the curtains' folds.
Think of breaking into rap, tap-dancing
down the darkened ward—
those tempting, softly gleaming floors—
all the time hearing again,
again, again, this rhyme:

> *Visiting hours are for those*
> *whose fathers aren't heroes*
> *like mine—flawed, old, in distress,*
> *but larger than life, yes,*
> *and, no, not ready for death.*

The starched nurse chorus echoes me
from their bright-white midnight can-can line,
but watching him muttering, lost
in the epic morphine scenery,
I stammer, falter, fluff my speech,
miss yet another cue.

Today's Lesson

This bed's a bitter pulpit, more a rack.
This strange breached gown, split surplice,
lacks his worn black cassock's dignity.
And no-one listens here. They bustle past
intent on their own rituals, all arcane to him:
the needle, monitor, that visionary light
they clamped onto his finger yesterday.
Now they can track him everywhere he goes—
it's plugged into the switchboard
and they can reach him quickly when it's time.
For what, he isn't sure, but he must think,
prepare. Where are they on the calendar—
Epiphany? Has the Creed been said?
His tongue is as dry as a bone,
but the words of his mouth will come
and they will be acceptable.

Withdrawal

I'm looking for my father's
little black dog.
The one that comes with me
for visiting hours, and jigs around,
up over all the sheets
and underneath the bed,
skittering happily
under the chair, around my legs.

He smiles, delighted, telling me
about the dog, a jolly chap,
how he will miss it and my company
when I get up to go.

I'm looking for my father
and that merry pitch-black dog.
It's late, but somewhere out there
in these polished wards
they're capering.
Old man and his best friend —
no drips, no morphine,
                    scarpered, off the leash.

Watch

Waking from his opium dreams
he looks at me. Child-like,
with steady curiosity, a calm surprise.
Both recognition and a questioning:
a girl reflected in his eyes, am I from his past,
from this life or the next?
He trusts me all the same, lets me hold his hand a while,
but turns his head to watch the doves
go about their own staccato busy-ness instead.
Away from the low-voiced murmur of the corridor,
the squeak of rubber soles, the swivelling wheels,
to the window's play, of spanned and folded wings.
Unconcerned by us, each strikes another pose—
swift flurry, skirmish; flutter, preen and strut—
as the line of sunlight rises to their ledge,
bright water, a slow and even flood.

Survivor

After the hospital, last year,
my father, shrunken in his chair,
looks like a vervet monkey now:
bearded, wizened, watching
with a pair of bright but tragic eyes.

Before, just months ago,
he'd hold the floor. But now he listens,
cocks his head at all the noise
and somehow seems more sly than wise.

Drip

There are bruises where the needles
tunnel under his thin skin.
The years of cortisone
extending and erasing him.
Dissolving father, wrestling
every breath—reach back to us,
resist. We are not ready for this
disappearance yet.

Cheynes-Stokes

All there is now is
this rise and fall, slow breakers,
crumbling cliffs, this breath.
Buffeted we cling and watch,
hold, unaware, our own.

The rasping, indrawn air—
the agonizing pause.
Hope at the gasp
then in its wake, despair.
Crouched unprepared
at this bleak border
to our separate unknowns.

Now in this no-man's-land,
I'm casting back, plumbing
every desolate interval.
And wondering:
what is it that they're thinking, seeking
in those moments till
another scanty second's share
is, briefly, possible?

And

And I was thinking in the breaking dawn,
my fingers on my father's precious skin:
so this is what a death is like.

And not just any death, I see that now: the good death
of a good man. How it takes a lifetime
to prepare for such a death.
And a lifetime after for the rest of us, recovering.
Trying not to botch what's left us of our own.

Afternoon

Waking, after the morning's bustle, after the tea,
celebration, sherry, sadness, sandwiches
and memories, passing around the endless trays
with all the pretty tea sets out, each patterned cup kept filled.

Our house has never seen such flowers: for five hot days
we've topped the vases up. Perhaps the perfume caused the slip—
or else the typing from the Prayer Book, choosing hymns—
but the words *the wedding* tumble often from my lips.

Good for a laugh, an easing, as we pass round scones:
everyone needs to say their piece, what he meant, what they'll miss
and I am as proud as I am sad, as busy and bright
as after a morning's church when the sermon had been his.

But now this: swimming upwards in the vague late afternoon,
the dismal light, I am swept by rage, a sudden flood,
at the murmur, muffled voices from the other room.
How dare they speak? Their mouths half-stuffed with all that's left

on the dreadful plates. So much useless breath, when we
have closed his open mouth, left gaping soft, as if asleep.
We bound it, gently, up. And now they mill and bleat like sheep.
What are they doing here, these fools? Their words are blasphemy.

That is *his* chair. They're dull, not blood enough. There is nothing
they can teach me with such blathering. I want to fly in,
make an end to all this waste and drive them, fiercely, out,
into the street. I wash my face. Boil water. Warm another pot.

One of the First Times After

One of the first times after: church,
and Easter Sunday. Good Friday
we had skipped: too soon, and too severe
a day. The days of our desertion,

no resurrection yet. If it were thus,
already, brethren, he would be
the one to hold the chalice to my lips:
long now since he had the strength for this.

Christmas last he struggled into vestments,
held the bread-filled paten up; the cup,
its taste of silver and sweet wine,
not quite enough to bind us,

fractious family, his slow diminishment
our own unhealing wound. He couldn't say
the blessing till he'd gone to pee:
we waited with our silent fears and prayers.

We far-flung sisters had just one more chance,
communion at his bed. Surrendered now,
a calm and grateful ring of chairs,
a loving colleague with the book,

my father's lines now his. Too weak
for words, propped up, he took it in—
a deeper feeding than the drip
we let him veto, swabbing out his mouth,

and letting, breath by breath, the spirit go.
Here, in the pew, a stoic threesome,
we bear the sermon and the intercession
made for us, bereaved; but leave—no, flee—

during the last verse of the closing
hymn. My mother, capable of facing
up to anything but sympathy,
and we too glad of the escape:

the congregation's sincere looks,
this mutilated Eucharist,
the wrong priest's hearty clasp.

The Paths of the Heavenly Bodies are Ordained

We are a house of women now,
six moons revolving planetless.

How he'd have smiled to read that line,
my dear astronomer—scanning his clear, adopted skies
through a prized telescope; seeing with faith.

Rejoicing in our orbit: daughters, wife,
the years of classes, congregations, rippling
from his life; of all this quietly proud.
Contented, centred, filled with certain hope.
Never, it seems, a moment's doubt.

Old Child

I cry so much I wake my mother up.
From the spare bedroom I can hear her stir.
Once was a time I would have given anything
for her to come to me, but now I smother it:
flee to the kitchen, wash my face,
heat milk, as though some bitter dream
or usual pain had woken me.

After Grief

Three drops of lavender in this water
is not balm enough.
Red thyme, a pungent antiseptic,
will not purge this day.
But I shall have it, scent and life.
I will not bathe in only salt and blood.

The Buried Butterfly

My iris purple skirt—
its silky swish—
was packed at first for partying in

but then the destination changed:
I checked in for a flight
towards his final journeying.

In that petal furl, with a beaded
butterfly to curb its wrap,
I helped to carry him,

a coffined husk,
across a patch of rocky ground
to dusty burying.

At last, a rest for him.
For me, the hollow pit of grief,
a body's emptying.

In a new uncompassed north
I dug a hole beneath a tree,
through softer soil. For memory,

these seeds: a bauble
and a photograph, snatched flowers,
the match's halo-ing.

There it must lie still
no longer winged:
just a scatter of beads melted
in the earth, and a rusted pin.

Again, or Dreams of My Father, Always Silent Now

They were silent, as the dead usually are
when they appear in our dreams . . .
W.G. SEBALD, *The Emigrants*

I

So soon, a dream.
Room upon room, a lucid house.
Walking from space to space
as though in painted light,
skirt-swirl, Jamesian enigmas.
And turned to me, that vanished face
and the sideways length of him
reflected in a doorway's long cheval.
Through a glass, darkly,
Hitchcockian papa,
not flesh, but watching me.
So soon. So incomplete.
But manna all the same.

II

Like old John Soane's
treasured Egyptian sarcophagus
my father's coffin stands,
plinthed ready for my offering.
In my hands I have some stolen blossoms
and some chosen stones.
And a book, a chunky paperback.
I lay it in there with the marble bust
which somehow is the man;
and then bethink myself.
I haven't read it yet. Must wait
and read it first before I let it go.

III

Small father perched
wry, mischievous
upon a shelf.
          Paternal elf,
tell me some truth.
But still no word.
Just a knowing twinkle,
infuriatingly benevolent,
as if to say—my words—
go work it out yourself.

IV

The undertakers. Hurry,
documents to sign, so much to organise
and as I turn the woman at the desk says, brightly:
'Oh, you won't be taking him along?'
O no! I have no space. The boot is full:
Salvation Army loot, clothes, garden tools;
look! curtains for the house. 'Ok, then,'
she concedes with a brisk wave of her pen.
'I'll have to freeze the body back—
three-quarter ways again.'

V

'Oh, dear,' my mother says:
'I think he's doing it again.
Dying, I mean.'
And so he is. In swaddling clothes,
a baby Daddy, early now for Christmas:
mummy-wrapped, his head, still large
and bearded, blooms from the cocoon.
Even in these throes,
the vestiges of cheerfulness.
And though I had to go through agonies—
briefer this time—to shepherd him,
on waking, I was thankful, still am,
always, to have seen that blessed face.

Night Skirmishes

> Don't leave bread or milk on the table
> At night: that attracts the dead.
> RILKE, *Sonnets to Orpheus*

Don't leave anything out, not without a lid.
Clear it away; the white cliff of the fridge is sanctuary.

Not just because determined lines of porter ants come track
across the kitchen's continent, from crumb to crumb.

Don't you know that I'm waging a war on cockroaches
in this house?! Her scolding holds a shudder back.

It's their soft scuffle on the old linoleum my mother fears:
their rusty armoured gloss, fine quivering antennae

undermine her house, a vision of decay. And we,
her pesky daughters, flitting in, and the absent dead —
so passive still — have proved no bloody use to her at all.

'And the Hyacinth's in Bloom—A Lovely Blue'

My mother's sudden pride in flowers—
how our desert garden grows
now that our father's gone,
now she has the time.

The shrouded mystery of bulbs,
veined globes of white:
the pale bulge of my father's ankle bone,
and the startling, naked nub—
the knot and pit where once his toe had been.

Dry April soil fed slowly
with these relics, what is left of him:
long-tended, worn-out,
all their pruned-back cankers quiet now.

After the amputation, bruising, weariness,
this stony rest, his paradise,
my mother's newfound flowers.